Dark Room

Sofia Costa

Presentation by *BookLeaf Publishing*

Web: www.bookleafpub.com

E-mail: info@bookleafpub.com

ISBN: 9789357441919

First edition 2023

*My little boy, partner and cats - may you
always bring the chaos.*

Awake

A grey light, enveloped the wakefulness
of the early night.
Controlled reassuring tones, suppressing
Panic and pained groans
A glimpse of a gleaming black puddle,
And a night broken with a gasping shuffle
Straight down the stairs, no time to change,
The ambulance is here
And a tiny eight year old heart
Already mourning without a loss
Begs a mother and unborn sister
To make it across

The child is fine

It was all fine
We had the sign - Mum and sister finally home
from hospital
The lost time a crime
Suddenly laughter
Curious frowns bleeding together in oranges and
browns
Giggles flowed through thorny gates
Days of milk drunkenness, and rapid growth
rates

But then the night would settle on my chest
Waiting abreast to open the door to further arrest
A puppet to the night
I'd awaken in the hallway
Downstairs
In the middle of brushing my teeth
Strung up to play with shadows underneath

The darkness started creeping into day.
The thoughts - so much harder to keep at bay.
They were stupid things. Repetitions of boring
sentences said in passing.

"Have you got your travel card? Have you got
your travel card? Have you got your travel
card?"
Shut up. Shut up. Shut up.

Next: count windows and doors.
On the way to school - Jesus Christ, you might
as well do the steps and floors.
No, that feels silly.
What is this madness?
Yearning for a day to be had without this.

I'm praying now.
Desperate times.
You'll call yourself an atheist later but here you
are
looking for the signs
This won't even be the last time you do this.

Good news. It doesn't work anyway.
There's no keeping the shadows at bay.

Light again, dark again, wait there's more.
Tonight I'll tackle the tiredness - that I'm sure.
Too late. The bed's wet.
Good job. Sponge and water it is.
You're getting quite good at this shame thing.

No matter. Everything is fine.
You're ten. You'll grow out of it - thanks doc.
All better. Oh wait, another shock. What is it this time?
No matter. You'll add borders and shape it to fit.
This is you now. You've grown into it.

Chillitto

A warrior, me
And probably a little feral
Orange and white - a raging rebel
No tummy rubs, I'm not about that
Not unless you want a gash down your arm -
stat!
Got places to be, dinners to be had
Wet food? I'm staying.
That doesn't sound too bad.
No one owns me, I'm not even playing
A bunch of groupies in the neighbourhood, is all
I'm saying
Ah man, I've come back with gashes, infected
You should see the fox though - caught him
unexpected
You took care of me though - that's cool
I've bought you a little mouse - why are you
running, you fool?
Fine, you're not ready
Next time I bring one back, I'll hold him steady
I'll stay here tonight - it's all nice and warm
I've heard there's going to be a bit of a deadly
rainstorm
Tonight. But what a cool April morn.
Right gotta go out for the usual track

I'm come back until I stop coming back
Don't wait up.

The Loon

You were called Princess
Perched on your human lap
Alone, but not the sole heiress
But, for you, raw chicken and a nap

Bright blue eyes
Prized jewels in the day
In darkness, say your goodbyes
Red - and evil to convey

A cloud
Springing and hopping
A cloud that might rain
String and bouncy balls allowed
Tiny dot to obtain

Paw over the servant's mouth
It's 3am, and royalty is hungry.
Pushing towards the door and south
Will only lead to chaotic fury,

Usually manifesting in a dirty protest.
Lovely little loon
No more midnight anti-food fests
Play us to your tune

Then came the little hairless human blob
Activating your love, your empathy
Charming each other with head bops
Meowing your sympathies.

"Princess"
A misjudgement on their part
Too enamoured to have seen
The rascal in your heart
My Luna, Queen.

My Magician

A rambunctious runt
Full of fire and spunk
We went to pick up our sister
But for you
Completely love drunk
A lightning spark
In the box you came
Fighting the limits of your world
In a black, white and ginger mane

A comforting purr
Tummy rubs all day
My stocky, furry blur
Green eyes ready to play

Nine lives depleted quick
But there's so many more
Somehow, a taste for bleach and white spirit!
On and off, sporadically sick
Life savings spirited away
But anything for this little
Magic

Not family? Not worth knowing!
Merlin, our scaredy cat

Loyal and somehow owing.
He'll tuck you into bed
Come on, read a book - he says
A book to rest my head.

My therapy and confession booth,
My first son
So much of our time is fearing
The day you're gone.

April

It's not a big event
Or something said
That sends me spiralling
It's the way the light flirts with a leaf
On a cold sunny morning
The swoosh of a car over the crisp tarmac
And the blue sky
Playfully dotted with clouds

Exposure is key - an expert spoke
I'm in luck
The weather is everywhere
A seasonal joke

I fucking hate April
A mocking month full of malice
Offering Springing hope like a poisoned chalice
Swiftly swooping in with its stupid grin
To birth unborn babies
Entrap wild cats and lose them to Hades
Arrest the innocent with hideous crimes
Hopping around bellflowers waiting for chimes

Bold

I'd argued my point meticulously
Timed and planned
A discussion on a mutual friend's Facebook
Your response, utterly bland
What a dick
Behold!
"Bold."

Meeting in a warm autumn evening
A mutual friend's birthday
Still a bit furious but
You spoke, normally
Excitedly
Behold
Bold

You asked for a drink with a lime in it
Can't remember what
I bought you a lime wedge
on top of a shot
An accident, I promise
You found it hilarious
No chance
Bold

Days were minutes and the winter brighter
Old Fashioneds and White Russians
FIFA, anger and laughter
A gentleman
Bastard
Bold

Charisma, strength and empathy
Look - I point, you shoot,
No chance, zombie
Gentleman bastard
Stats up
Bold

This game, we've almost clocked it
And then we level up again - new content
Too many potions, XP to be had
Start new game
Gentleman
Dad

Lockdown

Somehow, it started off exciting
Joyfully jousting belongings in lockers
Working from home - how thrilling!
Joy that would come back to mock us

Two weeks in - the air heavy
Staring at the same space,
And my partner
Virtual gatherings with a bevvy
The walls stifling
The snippets of sun through the window
Biting
A constant call in the ear
But a silence outside
No planes to hear
And the fear,
Like the walls were spiked and closing in
Two years of this and nothing certain,
Lives became worlds behind closed curtains

Waiting

We clung to the good news
Reading between non-existent lines
Turning to the world
With "phews" and contrived "fines"
Nothing but elaborate and forced pantomimes

Bad, good, worse news.
Phone calls with creeping doubt
Desperate doctors trying but without clues
Composed, pragmatic, yearning to shout
And the tears stream endlessly
As foreboding won out.

Fabric

Torn from the Fabric of the world
Ruthlessly from its Tapestry,
Unfinished stitching, frayed and cut off
Nice and neat.
Thrown in the scrapheap of tragedy

A scream at the back,
Cautious calm at the front
Both piercing denials of a script-less attack,
On a cloth now distorted and dull.
Absorbing tears
of mindless affront
But the reality of this bit of tat,
I can't yet willingly confront

Inadequate grief

Here we go - grief by zoom
Nothing like a bad connection
To unpack the dreariness of doom
Face to face gatherings if you want detention
Windows all the way down, now
Car rides need ventilation
Rules for you, not us, anyhow
You're the cause of isolation
A ten person limit, crowd
A part to play in this limitation
Sad, but no hugging allowed
Rules for some
Across our nation

Learned Helplessness

Control turns to water
Dripping screams into an abyss
It'll only take you as far as anything
Best give it a miss
Snap off those barbed wires
So tightly wound
Stop putting out fires
There will only be more
When you turn around
Focus on the things you can control
Park the things you can't
Any action you take - droll
Any achievement - scant
Let the world turn
The Politics eat itself
Soon it may be your turn
To undermine the wealth
Pick battles you can win
Everything in your stride
And there you'll find less heaviness
Heaviness, inside
They'll tell you this is maladaptive.
Yeah. But so what?
You're busy.
Busy, active.

Pandemic Pandemonium

A fear there will be no legacy of him and you
A story too important to end without biological
memory
So you grow life when time has stopped
Wash your hands
Anti-bacterial wipes to your shopping
Wear a mask, religiously, excessive bleaching
Hoping
That neither of you die
That this isn't just a hiccup
A shrug, a sigh
But a bulletin bellowed by bold bards
Twisting to the test of time
Heard from mountains high

Push

Zero to sixty
Short, snappy
Sustained and sneaky.
Bones tear apart
Heart drops
Dismay
This is only the start?

A melody of Shakespearean plays
Acts one…two…three
Comedy, ironic tragedy, machiavelli
What cosmic betrayal

I trained for this
Breath, breath, breath
Two hours of no progress
The cosmos…. hilarious!

Mentally throwing chairs
Midwives giving me their wares
Clackety-shush of the gas and air
I'm saying hello and suppressing glares

Gas is out.
New drugs please

Not part of the plan.
Dark ages
Lights out.

Scream. Blackout. Scream.

And between
A loving father writes the notes of history
Taking in the scene

"Listen to your body"
Body is telling me to push
"Don't push".
Alright, copy.

37 hours - exhaustion hits.
Doc. Now.
"One more push"
No. Now.

Here

The shock of life hit us both

Warm
Grey and wrinkly
The weight and movements - familiar
The tentative stretching of your hand
Testing, curious
The uncoordinated kicking of your feet
Stunned, furious

But no longer hooked under my rib

You look at me
And the moment
Freezes.

I see you.
A snowglobe of you and me
Suspended in time

Before it races

Insidious Kindness

Move.
Stop lazing about
You're a mother now - no excuses
So what if it feels like
Your insides are falling out
What
Do you want me to do about it?
Sore and vulnerable? Grow up
Let's sort that dignity out real quick
To be a mother - you aren't fit.

Quit.
But clean your piss and blood off the floor -

Calm
Let's clean you up - no shame
You've done a difficult thing
Today.
What's his name?
Ah beautiful - no you're not
A child.
He'll be charmer
Truth be told
This is wild, but relatively mild

Shift over - checking in
You're doing great
Don't panic.
Remember, skin to skin.
Ah look, he's cooing!
Truth be told
It's confusing
Nobody knows what they're doing.

Routine

25

Turn on the shower
For a split second
An embryo protected by its walls
But then
Routine or cower
More milk!
The baby calls

How was there ever time to think?
To eat, sleep
Drink.
No time to wake up
Too exhausted to blink
Turn the shower off
Routine
Or sink.

(In)equity

Drink coffee cold
Wipe crumbs from my son's head
Hiding away waiting to be told
Chores to do before bed

Sleep when he sleeps
Who will pump, clean bottles, fold
The hundred tiny items piled in heaps
Energy depleted, replaced by a cold

No sick days here
Not for anyone it seems
One improving a career
One cleaning sick up while suppressing fevers
And dreams

This is a 24 hour
Extra curricular activity
Love and sleep devour
But short term pause for the proclivity for
creativity
He's growing by the hour

Motherhood, I thought

I thought it would be easier
I thought the love of the thing would make
things breezier.
Things aren't a breeze
And there are things you never accounted for
The dreaded right-into-your-mouth sneeze
His dribble up your nose
A nappy of Weetabix and solid peas

I thought I'd be stricter,
I thought I'd have the will to say no to the little
trickster.

I thought I'd be less tired
I thought I'd have more time and be constantly
inspired
There's no real inspiration
It's all reflex and iteration
With people who know better,
Always providing an explanation
But innateness kicks in with altruistic
preservation

I thought I'd love him - yes

But I thought, at least, there would be something
I could easily suppress
The love is a breeze
And there are things you don't account for
The love grows as leaves grow on trees
You love him, you love him and then there's
Somehow more
Even when he gets on your last nerve
You'll love him more tomorrow than ever before

Words

Plucking familiar words
From little snowflakes
Falling on curious hands
Moulding and constructing them
Into special little lands

There's snow in the garden - look!
Grow-ing snow
Ah no, it fell from the sky
Can't take credit for that one, sweets
Re-really, really haaaai

Bobble hat
Wobbly hands
Wobble cups
Cup-pah tea
Here's a building block on a coaster
Cup-pah
tea

Throw-ing wah-tah
Very close - that's a shower, sweets
Build a tow-wah
What a big tower! Not too high
Ro-bot tow-wah

Nor-mun
Norman, the robot tower to the sky!

Outta space
Planets of the soula sista
And you the centre
What comes after Mercury, sweets?
Mainly..... Jupit-ah

Cud-dle mummy
Always
My cuddle and my wow
Anything for my twinkling star
My very awake
Little owl

We used to be close

United in all things - film to fears
Riding the waves of a mother's love and woes
Saturday morning cartoons and evening gigs
Interests rarely opposed

A sea between us
Where we build homes
Walls, broken down by a sudden sadness
Stuck inside virtual phone calls

Life moves on again
Updates timeboxed to birthdays and
Christmasses
Questions, once ample, sparse and incurious
An air of annoyance at my stresses
The microaggressions, misogyny and
motherhood messes

Huffs and sighs
A new risk at every interaction
Rolling of the eyes
The holding back of diatribes
As I realise too late
And a bit embarrassed
I'm no longer part of your faction

www.ingramcontent.com/pod-product-compliance
Lightning Source LLC
LaVergne TN
LVHW021329200726

843509LV00014B/2460